R0061821617

04/2012

FOOTBALL:
A SHORT HISTORY

Matthew Taylor

Published in Great Britain in 2011 by Shire Publications Ltd, Midland House, West Way, Botley, Oxford OX2 0PH, United Kingdom.

44-02 23rd Street, Suite 219, Long Island City, NY 11101, USA.

E-mail: shire@shirebooks.co.uk   www.shirebooks.co.uk

A CIP catalogue record for this book is available from the British Library.

Shire Library no. 649.   ISBN-13: 978 0 74781 052 0

Matthew Taylor has asserted his right under the Copyright, Designs and Patents Act, 1988, to be identified as the author of this book.

Designed by Tony Truscott Designs, Sussex, UK and typeset in Perpetua and Gill Sans.

Printed in China through Worldprint Ltd.

11 12 13 14 15   10 9 8 7 6 5 4 3 2 1

COVER IMAGE
The FA cup final between Manchester United and Aston Villa under way at Wembley Stadium, 1957.

TITLE PAGE IMAGE
Welsh international John Charles was one of British football's most successful exports. Moving from Leeds United to Juventus in 1957, he won three *Serie A* championships with the Turin side and became fondly remembered by local supporters as 'King John'.

CONTENTS PAGE IMAGE
London Transport posters played an important part in advertising key matches in the capital. Underground posters for the FA Cup in the 1920s and 1930s became iconic and are sold in the twenty-first century as posters and other merchandise.

ACKNOWLEDGEMENTS
Thanks to John Hutchinson for generous use of the Leicester City FC Digital Archive, Max Dunbar and The Everton Collection Charitable Trust, Paul Smith at the Thomas Cook Archives and Victoria Hogarth at the Bridgeman Art Library. I would also like to thank my colleagues at the International Centre for Sports History and Culture at De Montfort University and James Panter, Bharti Mistry, Colin Richdale and Anne McLoughlin. And finally, thanks to Alex and Thomas. This book is for them.

Illustrations and photographs are acknowledged as follows:

Bridgeman Art Library, page 6 (bottom); The Everton Collection Charitable Trust, pages 11 (top), 13, 36 (bottom), 39, 42 (left), 43 (top), 48 (bottom), 50; Getty Images, page 30; Leicester City FC Digital Archive, pages 9, 11 (bottom), 14, 16 (bottom), 17 (top), 19, 21 (top and bottom), 26 (top left and bottom), 28 (top and bottom), 29 (bottom), 32 (top left), 33 (bottom), 34, 35 (bottom right), 36 (top), 38 (top), 40, 42 (right), 45 (bottom left), 47, 48 (top left), 51 (top and bottom), 54, 55, 57, 60 (bottom), 61; Mary Evans Picture Library, page 4; The National Archives, page 37; National Football Museum, Preston, UK/The Bridgeman Art Library, pages 3, 7, 8, 10, 17 (bottom); Thomas Cook Archive, pages 24, 33 (top), 52; Wingfield Sporting Gallery/The Bridgeman Art Library, cover image.

All other material is from the author's collection.

CONTENTS

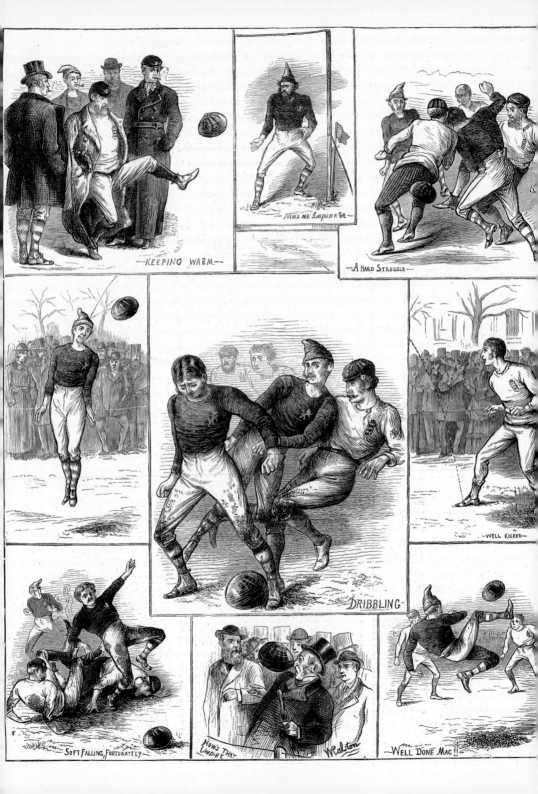

— KEEPING WARM —

— NEMO ME IMPUNE &c —

— A HARD STRUGGLE —

— WELL KICKED —

DRIBBLING —

— SOFT FALLING, FORTUNATELY —

HOW'S THAT UMPIRE

W Ralston

— WELL DONE MAC !! —

ORIGINS OF ASSOCIATION FOOTBALL

A SSOCIATION FOOTBALL had its origins in the chaotic and unregulated forms of folk football popular throughout Britain from the Middle Ages. These games became embedded in local community life, uniting aristocratic patrons and working-class participants in a raucous and often violent form of ritualised play. As industrialisation and urbanisation gathered pace, traditional recreations of all types found themselves increasingly under threat. Restrictions on space and time – through the enclosure of common land and the imposition of new working practices and disciplinary regimes – combined with the active disapproval of magistrates, police and local reformers to limit the frequency and prominence of folk football.

In 1801, Joseph Strutt commented that popular football 'of late seems to have fallen into disrepute, and is all but little practised'. It may have been marginalised but, contrary to Strutt's view, it was not killed off. Indeed, the evidence for the resilience and gradual transformation of folk football in the early to mid-nineteenth century is compelling. In Kingston-upon-Thames, for example, attempts to prohibit the annual Shrove Tuesday match in 1799 proved unsuccessful. Three players were taken into custody and the crowd were read the proclamation of the Riot Act. But the crowd failed to disperse and no troops arrived, allowing the competitors to rescue their fellow players from the local prison. In a letter to the Home Secretary, the magistrates lamented that 'the Mob' had got the better of them and correctly predicted that the game would henceforth 'be carried on to a greater height than it has ever been'.

Subsequent attempts to suppress the Kingston match also failed and it was still being played into the 1840s. The traditional annual Dorking football match was likewise taking place on the streets of the Surrey town as late as 1888. In pockets of the country, local versions of football survived, often as annual events, adapting to changed circumstances but retaining many of the characteristics of earlier periods.

Elsewhere, traditional forms of football underwent a slow but steady process of modernisation. There is evidence of matches between teams of

Opposite:
An illustration of the first match between national teams representing Scotland and England. Played in November 1872 at the West of Scotland Cricket Club, the game drew a crowd of a few thousand and finished goalless.

Contents page from *The Book of Football*, published by the Amalgamated Press in 1906. It featured articles on training, and the economics of football as well as a series of short essays on the early history of the game and on 'famous' clubs.

THE
BOOK OF FOOTBALL
A COMPLETE HISTORY AND RECORD
OF THE
ASSOCIATION AND RUGBY GAMES

Photo by R. W. THOMAS,
41, Cheapside, London, E.C.

Copyright—HUDSON & KEARNS,

Charles Alcock was a key figure in the organisation of football in its early days. He was secretary of the FA for twenty-five years, organised and played in the first England-Scotland international and was the driving force behind the creation of the FA Cup.

equal but variable numbers being arranged for stake money as early as the 1830s and 1840s. Many were based around public houses. Challenges were often made, and rules and terms arranged, via announcements in local as well as prominent national newspapers such as *Bell's Life in London*. On Good Friday 1838, for instance, a contest between eleven men from Leicester and eleven from Derby took place at the Leicester cricket ground, with the winners planning to challenge 'an equal number from any town in England' for a £25 stake. Team size and rules varied considerably but referees and umpires were common and the play was often more skilled and less violent than earlier descriptions of 'mob' football suggest.

One city in particular was notable for its burgeoning football culture during the 1850s and 1860s: Sheffield. The city became important first of all because it could boast the oldest and one of the most influential football clubs of the time. Sheffield Football Club was formed on 24 October 1857 by a number of players attached to the cricket club at Bramall Lane. It was initially a socially exclusive organisation targeting 'the young gentlemen' of the city and run by prominent local entrepreneurs, merchants and professional men. The elevated social standing of the club's membership meant that it retained an influential position in the city's football scene as other clubs were quickly formed. Also significant was the club's code of

Famous English footballers of 1881, from the *Boy's Own* magazine. The picture features association and rugby football players, at a time when the two codes were vying for supremacy in many parts of Britain.

FAMOUS ENGLISH FOOTBALL PLAYERS. 1881.

Thomas Hemy's painting of a league match between Sunderland and Aston Villa is one of the first artistic representations of association football. The painting features the two leading professional teams of the 1890s, who between them won eight Football League championships during the decade.

play, the 'Sheffield Rules', which was widely adopted by emerging teams in the city and beyond.

During the 1860s, football was probably more highly developed in Sheffield than in any other part of Britain. Over a dozen clubs were active by 1862 and matches between Sheffield FC and their chief rivals, Hallam FC, drew considerable local interest. Although games were arranged primarily for players rather than spectators, attendances sometimes reached several hundred. The influence of Sheffield football spread further via representative matches with teams from Nottingham, Glasgow and London, among others. For these reasons, the 'steel city' could justifiably lay claim to being the first genuine powerhouse of organised football.

At around the same time, football was also emerging as a popular recreation within the nation's public schools and universities. Dating back to the sixteenth century, public school football was, like the games played outside school gates, initially rather rough and unrefined. Each school had its own distinctive game shaped by its local environment, buildings and facilities. Lack of space often dictated a game's characteristics. At Charterhouse and

A photograph taken at Leicester Fosse's Filbert Street ground in the 1890s. Attendances were relatively small and the spectators lined the pitch only a few rows deep.

Westminster, football initially took place in the restricted space of the cloisters and play was characterised by individual dribbling. No such physical limitations existed at Harrow, where there was a large playing field. But poor drainage made the use of a heavy ball essential, with the rules encouraging movement to offset the potential for static scrimmages in the heavy mud.

Unregulated and violent forms of football were characteristic of the general disorder in the late-eighteenth and early-nineteenth-century public schools. By the 1850s and 1860s, however, football had become central to a reformed public school system based on discipline, morality and manliness. Forward-thinking masters recognised the potential value of the game in meeting desired practical and educational objectives. On one level, it could occupy the spare time and energy of boys who might otherwise drift into more disruptive or immoral activities. But football and other games were also considered vital elements of the character-building agenda characteristic of Victorian public school education. Through playing football, the sons of the upper and upper-middle classes could learn about teamwork, courage and toughness. As an 1864 Royal Commission on the public schools recognised, the cricket and football fields were 'not merely places of amusement'; they were instrumental in forming 'some of the most valuable social qualities and manly virtues'. Football, it was thought, could help mould boys into gentlemen and future leaders.

To achieve this, the chaotic games of the past had to be organised and regulated. Written rules were an essential part of this process. The length of matches and the size of the playing area were also limited and the number of players in teams reduced and equalised. Interest in football spread as the schoolboys took their versions of football with them to university and beyond. Conflicts between the alumni of different schools led to attempts to

Freemasons Tavern Great Queen Street Lincolns Inn Fields.

Freemasons' Tavern in Lincoln's Inn Fields, London, was the venue for a meeting of captains and representatives of London clubs in October 1863. The Football Association was founded and over subsequent months a common set of rules was agreed.

arrive at common rules that all could adhere to. Rules were framed in various contexts and at regular intervals. All failed to catch on before a group of undergraduates at Cambridge University agreed on a new set of guidelines in 1863.

Similar advances were being made inside and outside elite educational institutions but the so-called 'Cambridge Rules' of 1863 were to have particular significance. At the same time as the Cambridge students were framing their rules, the representatives of a number of London suburban clubs were meeting for a similar purpose. Some favoured a game that promoted carrying the ball and hacking (kicking opponents' shins) but the existence of the 'Cambridge Rules' helped the proponents of dribbling to carry the debate. The first set of rules of the nascent Football Association (FA), enshrined in December 1863, therefore provided the basis for the development of two distinct football codes. The supporters of running with the ball and hacking, led by the Blackheath club, resigned immediately, establishing their own Rugby Football Union (RFU) in 1871. Those who remained set about the tricky task of extending the authority of the FA and the newly codified sport of association football.

They struggled at first. Although 'football' in general increased in popularity during the 1860s and 1870s, distinct and competing versions of the game continued to complicate the picture. In addition to the FA and RFU rules, a number of local codes of football were recorded as being played into the mid-1870s. Some clubs chose a particular code and stuck with it but others were more flexible, switching between codes as circumstances, opposition and fashion demanded.

The FA's authority over the dribbling version of the game emerged slowly, aided significantly

Nick Ross was one of professional football's first stars. He played for Preston North End and Everton in the 1880s and 1890s. The sports journalist James Catton described him in the 1920s as 'the most brilliant back of his day, if not all time'.

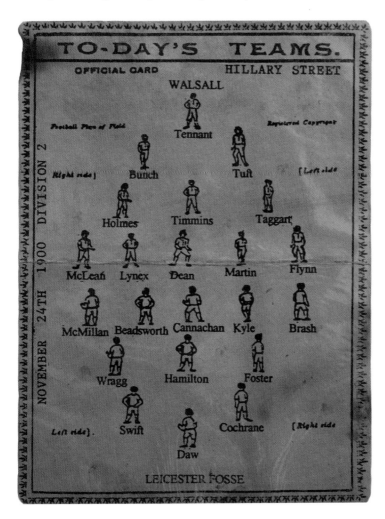

Most teams from the 1890s to the 1920s adopted a 2-3-5 formation. The wing half backs marked the opposing wingers, the full-backs covered the centre, and the centre half was expected to move between defence and attack.

A Football League handbook from the 1897–8 season. With two divisions and thirty-two clubs, the Football League was well established as the pre-eminent league competition in England and Wales. Its chief rival up to the First World War was the Southern League.

by the support and influence of the Sheffield clubs in the provinces. The decisive moment, however, came with the success of its own challenge cup competition. Inaugurated in 1871–2, the FA Cup was initially dominated by clubs consisting of ex-public schoolboys from London and the Home Counties. Royal Engineers, Wanderers, Old Etonians and Oxford University monopolised the first seven finals but the net gradually widened geographically and socially. By the early 1880s, the best provincial clubs were progressing to the later stages of the competition. Lancashire clubs were most successful. Blackburn Rovers were defeated finalists in 1882 but won the competition in 1884, 1885 and 1886; local rivals Blackburn Olympic recorded the first northern victory in 1883, beating the Old Etonians in a final described by one newspaper as a clash between 'patricians' and 'plebeians'.

A combination of factors led association football to become the most popular sport among the working classes in Britain during the last quarter of the nineteenth century. Increases in wages and free time were an essential prerequisite, helping to create potential leisure consumers who could find the time to play or watch their favourite sports. As the popularity of watching football increased, individual entrepreneurs decided to enclose grounds, charge entrance money and build new stadiums. The idea was already well established in sports such as cricket, athletics and horse racing. It was successfully applied to football (of all codes) and by the early 1870s many of the most prominent clubs had fenced off their playing fields and built gates at which spectators had to pay to enter.

Football had arrived as a spectator sport. Attendances were highest in Scotland and the Midlands and north-west of England. Six thousand were

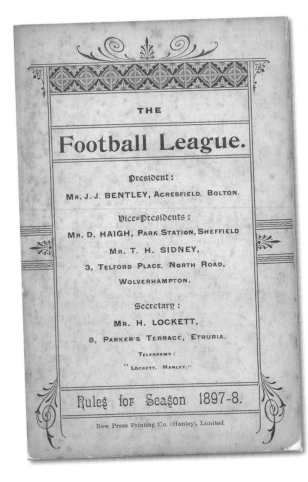

present at the 1882 FA Cup final at the Oval in London but 20,000 spectators were reported to have watched Darwen's clash with Blackburn Rovers a couple of months earlier. Clubs were anxious to secure the services of the best players. There was a widespread recognition that, in order to maintain the support of the emerging football consumer, clubs had to ensure that the team won and/or the quality of play was good. After a poor start to the 1884–5 season, for instance, the influential Manchester weekly *Athletic News* advised the Blackburn Rovers committee that they would 'not only lose a lot of engagements, but they will find a considerable falling off of gate receipts' if the team was not improved. In such circumstances, signing talented players became essential to both sporting success and financial security. The conditions for the rise of professional football were now in place.

The Everton FC Board of Directors, c. 1906. Most directors in football's early days wielded considerable power. They bought and sold players, selected the teams and monitored the performance and behaviour of their playing staff closely.

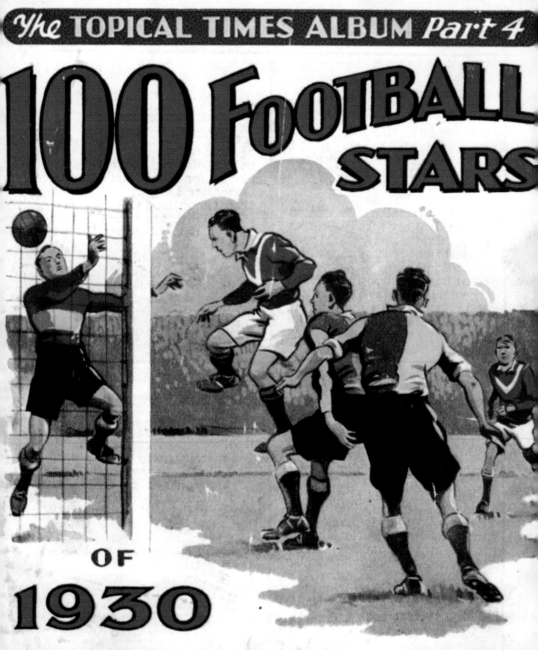

THE TOPICAL TIMES ALBUM *Part 4*

100 FOOTBALL STARS

OF
1930

IN · ACTUAL · CLUB · COLOURS
FULL · BIOGRAPHIES

AMATEURS AND PROFESSIONALS

AMATEURISM was a crucial aspect of Victorian and Edwardian sport. It was a complex phenomenon that embodied a particular set of principles that opposed making a profit on, or gambling on, sport; an ethos that emphasised sportsmanship and fair play; and an administrative structure based on the creation of voluntary national bodies to regulate sport. Amateurism was also infused with class connotations. Amateurs were often former public school men with the necessary private means to devote their time to playing or promoting sport. The ideal amateur was also a gentleman. Working-class men could be amateurs but they rarely embraced the wider gentlemanly values of playing with dignity, self-control, effortless style and courage.

Football was run by gentleman amateurs from the beginning. We have seen that it was mainly young public school and Oxbridge-educated men who founded the Football Association (FA) in 1863 and they continued to dominate the game's governing body for many decades. A significant number were from aristocratic backgrounds and had attended high-status schools such as Eton, Harrow, Charterhouse and Westminster. A fair few were titled and employed in upper-middle-class professional occupations. At the very top of the hierarchy were men such as Major Francis Marindin, an Eton-educated vicar's son from Shropshire, and Arthur (later Lord) Kinnaird, another Etonian and a merchant banker who later became Lord High Commissioner of the Church of Scotland. Kinnaird was one of the game's earliest stars. A flamboyant character, he appeared in seven FA Cup finals between 1876 and 1883, famously celebrating victory in 1882 by standing on his head in front of the Oval pavilion. Between them Marindin and Kinnaird monopolised the FA presidency from 1874 until 1923.

On the field, the balance of power between amateurs and professionals was changing rapidly. The Old Etonians' 1-0 victory over Blackburn Rovers in 1882, complete with Kinnaird's extravagant celebration, proved to be the last time an amateur club was to win the FA Cup. As football became the preferred sport of the labouring classes, the dominance of the gentleman amateur footballer waned. The decision to legalise

Opposite:
Topical Times was one of a number of publications that popularised the footballer's image by publishing individual profiles, photographs and biographies of 'star' players.

Right: A portrait of Lord Kinnaird, a leading amateur player in the 1870s and one of the foremost administrators in English football before the First World War. Kinnaird played in nine FA Cup finals and won five winners' medals.

Opposite, top: A pair of football boots from the inter-war years. Early boots were made of solid leather, with high sides around the ankles and toughened leather in the toecaps. Good boots were essential equipment for the aspiring amateur as well as the professional.

professionalism in England in 1885 was a significant blow. By deciding to control rather than prohibit the professional, the FA avoided a potential split in its ranks but doomed the amateur to a precarious future. A separate FA Amateur Cup was established in 1893 but it, too, soon became dominated by working-class teams, mainly from the north-east of England.

One or two amateur clubs stood firm against the professional tide. Glasgow's Queen's Park, the oldest club in Scotland, was staunchly amateur. It was the most

Right: The styles of football kits varied considerably. Some shirts had collars, other did not; some were laced up at the neck while others had buttons like regular shirts or vests. Goalkeepers (such as George Strong) tended to wear heavier polo-neck jerseys.

Presented with Topical Times.

HARRY R. HOOPER,
Sheffield United F.C.

WILLIAM COBLEY,
Aston Villa F.C.

GEORGE J. STRONG,
Portsmouth F.C.

successful side in Scotland during the 1880s, winning the Scottish Cup five times and reaching two English cup finals, but it refused to join the new Scottish Football League in 1890 or to embrace professionalism when it was legalised there in 1893. In England, the beacon of the gentleman's amateur game was the Corinthian FC. Founded in 1882 by N. L. Jackson, assistant secretary of the FA, the Corinthians were intended to represent the very best ex-public school and university talent. The team had no home ground and refused to enter cup and league competitions. But they were more than able to hold their own against the best professional teams of the day. In 1884 they thrashed the FA Cup holders Blackburn Rovers 8-1 and five years later defeated Preston North

Below:
A photograph of a Corinthians team from 1895. Described by one of their first historians as 'England's greatest amateur team', the Corinthians were applauded in amateur circles for playing an open game that was hard but fair.

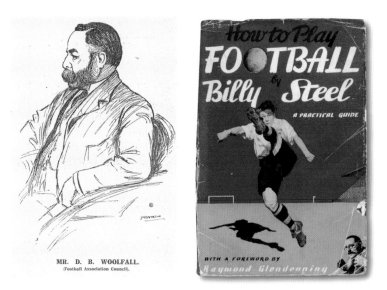

Right: A portrait of D. B. Woolfall, a prominent member of the FA Council from 1883 until his death in 1918. Woolfall was FA treasurer and a leading advocate of amateur football. He was also president of FIFA between 1906 and 1918.

Far right: Instructional books written by professional and amateur footballers were common from the late nineteenth century. Billy Steel's *How to Play Football* (with a foreword by radio commentator Raymond Glendenning) appeared in 1948.

MR. D. B. WOOLFALL.
(Football Association Council).

End, the first holders of the league and cup double, 5-0. Between 1882 and 1907, Corinthian players took one third of all England caps in the annual matches against Scotland, while in the 1884 and 1885 contests with Wales the whole England team were Corinthians.

By the inter-war years, however, amateurs had been all but swept away at the elite level. The defenders of pure amateurism continued to bemoan their marginalisation and rail against the evils of 'business football' and 'spectatorism' but the plain fact was that on the whole professional footballers and teams played to a higher standard. The amateur game underwent a short-lived revival after the Second World War as the popularity of football in general soared. The FA Amateur Cup final between Bromley and Romford drew a crowd of 93,000 to Wembley Stadium in 1949, with a record 100,000 attending two years later. The winners on that occasion were the joint Oxford and Cambridge University team Pegasus, formed a few years earlier as the new standard bearers of the gentleman amateur in football. But it was becoming impossible to maintain the amateur–professional distinction and in 1974 the FA finally did away with it entirely.

The first footballers to be paid to play were the so-called 'Scotch Professors'. Regarded as the most skilled and technical of early players, they developed a distinct style based on sharp, short passing and combination between team-mates. From the 1870s many moved to wealthier clubs in England, where their talents were in considerable demand. Professionalism was banned so they were found convenient employers by the directors or patrons of the clubs for which they played. One of the first football migrants was a Glaswegian, James Lang, who, despite losing the sight of an eye working in the shipyards on the Clyde, first played for the Wednesday club in Sheffield in 1876. He was nominally employed at a knife-making firm owned by a member of the Wednesday committee but this may have been a cover to justify his presence in the city, as he seems to have spent most of his working day reading the newspaper.

It took some time to establish the status and reputation of the profession. Footballers in the late Victorian and Edwardian era were not always well regarded and were often dismissed as mercenaries, gamblers and drinkers. It did not help that in the 1880s leading players such as Sheffield's Bill Mosforth had been willing to change sides before a match for 'ten bob and free drinks all week'. Transfer regulations were tightened in the 1890s, and the imposition in 1901 of a maximum wage of £4 per week meant that there was less incentive to move club for financial gain. But the notion of the 'one-club' man who stayed loyal to his home-town team for his entire career was always less common than is sometimes assumed. 'The days of long service seem to be dying fast', wrote one observer of the football scene in 1928;

Early training techniques were often rudimentary, involving sprinting and lapping the track. Relatively little time was spent with the ball on improving skills and honing technique. The Leicester City players are (left to right), George Carr, Sid Bishop, Arthur Chandler and John Duncan.

Right: Special training at a seaside resort the week before an important cup tie was an established part of the occupational culture of British football. It gave players a chance to relax and train away from the normal working environment.

a Day With GRIMSBY TOWN in SPECIAL TRAINING

After breakfast a look at the news—QUIGLEY, LUMBY, TWEEDY, VINCENT.

Dominoes passes the half-hour before lunch for BUCK and CRAVEN.

Leaving their hotel for a practice game—BESTALL, CRAVEN, TWEEDY, DYSON, QUIGLEY, KELLY, HODGSON, LUMBY, Manager W. SPENCER.

Give him a ball and he's happy — JACKIE COULTER.

"Up to it!" The practice match was a lovely affair—BETMEAD, LUMBY, COULTER, BESTALL, VINCENT, TWEEDY, KELLY, HODGSON.

Manager SPENCER does his stuff.

Brine baths—where you can't sink!

Below:
A caricature of 'Dixie' Dean, the most famous footballer of the 1920s and 1930s. Dean was a prodigious goalscorer, notching up a record of sixty goals for Everton during the 1927–8 season.

PLAYER'S CIGARETTES.

W.R. (DIXIE) DEAN.

'This is the age of transfers.' Indeed 338 professionals moved clubs in England during the 1934–5 season alone.

That some professionals drank too much and behaved badly is without question. The problem was so bad at Aston Villa in 1900 that a private detective was employed to spy on the players away from the club. The Scotland international Jimmy Cowan was found to be drunk '2–3 times a week', while team-mate Jimmy Crabtree admitted drinking with Cowan days before a league match. The image was reinforced by the popularity of characters like the music-hall comic Harry Weldon's 'Stiffy the Goalkeeper', who kept a jug of beer behind his goal and was susceptible to bribery by outside betting interests.

As football matured as a profession, however, standards of behaviour improved. So too did the image associated with the 'pro'. The players' own trade union, established in 1907, played a key role in helping to improve pay and conditions of service. As early as 1923, the football bureaucrat Charles Sutcliffe suggested that the 'standing' of the professional had 'risen by leaps and bounds. The old pot-walloping, whisky-swiping player has substantially gone out of the game.' Another writer described the 1920s professional as 'a clean-living, healthy sportsman'. Newspapers and magazines increasingly portrayed footballers as respectable professional men: well-dressed, clean-living and dependable. The ghosted autobiographies of 'star' players published in the 1940s and 1950s underlined the impression of footballers as exemplary models of manhood and sportsmanship. To their readers, Eddie Hapgood, Stanley Matthews and Tom Finney were revealed as self-confident, proud professionals, but importantly as gentlemen too.

The material rewards for playing professionally did not always reflect this elevated status. For sure, most footballers were considerably better off than if they had worked in the local mill or gone down the pits. Jerry Dawson recalled earning £15 per week (with bonuses) for Glasgow Rangers in 'the palmy days of football' during the 1930s. 'In the circumstances of the time we were millionaires', he admitted. Tom Finney likewise remembered his £8 a week with £2 win bonus as 'a fortune' and Stan Cullis wrote in his autobiography that by the age of twenty-one he had 'saved enough, without stirring myself, to buy two semi-detached houses or a medium-sized car twice over had I so wanted'.

By the early 1950s, however, the comparison was no longer with industrial workers but with other entertainers. Why, it was argued, should the most talented footballers not be free to earn the types of salary open to the stars of stage and screen? The pressure for change eventually proved too much for the football authorities and in 1961 the restrictive maximum wage law was abolished.

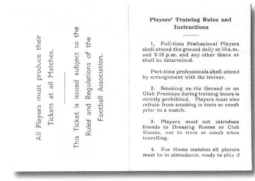

Players' Training Rules and Instructions

1. Full-time Professional Players shall attend the ground daily at 10 a.m. and 2-15 p.m. and any other times as shall be determined.

Part-time professionals shall attend by arrangement with the trainer.

2. Smoking on the Ground or on Club Premises during training hours is strictly prohibited. Players must also refrain from smoking in train or coach prior to a match.

3. Players must not introduce friends to Dressing Rooms or Club Rooms, nor to train or coach when travelling.

4. For Home matches all players must be in attendance, ready to play if

Professional footballers were subject to similar systems of control and discipline as in other occupations. This set of rules and instructions dates from the 1950s.

The famous Blackpool, Stoke City and England winger Stanley Matthews. A model professional, Matthews looked after his body as a tradesman did his tools and was still playing professionally in 1965 at the age of fifty.

Within a matter of months Fulham's Johnny Haynes became the first £100 a week footballer and the earnings of the elite rose gradually over subsequent decades. We should remember though that life was never so comfortable on the lower rungs of the professional ladder. George Best was said to be earning around £2,000 a week in 1970 but a significant proportion of Third and Fourth Division players

Above: Golf was a popular pastime among footballers. Some clubs encouraged their employees to play as a form of relaxation. A number of professionals also played cricket, some to a high level, during the summer months.

Right: Footballers were frequently portrayed by the specialist sporting and the national press as fashionable and respectable professional men during the 1930s.

THE BEST DRESSED PLAYERS

TED CATLIN (Sheff. Wednesday)—Likes his materials hefty and very much built to order.

BERRY NIEUWENHYS (Liverpool)—Subdued good quality materials. Always looks well cared for and well turned out.

HARRY HOLDCROFT (Preston North End)—Always spruce but conventional.

GEORGE AINSLEY (Leeds Utd.)—Unconventional, comfortable and colourful.

FRANK SWIFT (Manchester City)—Has a good eye for blending the colours.

PERCY GROSVENOR (Leicester City)—Sophisticated taste.

LEN BUTT (Blackburn Rovers)—Bright dresser, likes light, colourful effects.

BOB STUART (Middlesbrough)—Crisp and dapper.

Left: A class of apprentices being given a lesson in the laws of football at Blackburn Rovers in the late 1960s. The football authorities for many years resisted the idea that players could be taught to improve their understanding of the game.

Below: Fourth Division Darlington had a complicated incentive system of bonus payments for its players. Neville Chapman (top row, second from left) was paid a basic wage of £25 per week in 1967 but could make more if home attendances rose above six thousand or if the club was placed in the top half of the division.

were on basic wages of less than £45 a week. The records of Fourth Division Darlington reveal that £25 or £22 per week was common at around the same time; injuries and the economic recession also meant that careers could be short and precarious.

CLUBS AND COMMUNITIES

FOOTBALL was built upon the peculiarly tight-knit community identities characteristic of British working-class life. Local teams could provide a focus for community consciousness, linking together disparate groups of individuals in a common cause every week. Yet as the neighbourhoods and communities that they served changed over the course of the twentieth century, many clubs struggled to adapt. Indeed, some became increasingly distanced and estranged from the very communities whose names they bore.

Football clubs originated from a number of community associations and local institutions. Schools, churches and workplaces were among the most common. Famous examples of grammar and state school origins include the old boys of Wyggeston School in Leicester who formed Leicester Fosse (later renamed Leicester City) in 1884 and the 1879 foundation of the Sunderland and District Teachers' Association club, which later became Sunderland FC. Well-known former church or Sunday-school teams include Aston Villa (Villa Cross Wesleyan Chapel), Everton (St Domingo's Church Sunday School) and Southampton (St Mary's Church). And the workplaces of Singer's cycle factory, the Lancashire and Yorkshire Railway Company and the munitions factory in Woolwich provided the environment for the forerunners of Coventry City, Manchester United and Arsenal respectively. Others, such as Derby County, Preston North End and Tottenham Hotspur, emerged from existing cricket clubs.

More numerous than all these examples, however, were teams based around the suburb, neighbourhood or street. In Blackburn in the late 1870s a number of clubs had grown around street teams and still bore their names: Red Row Star, Gibraltar Street, Cleaver Street Rovers, for example. The same was true of the Stirling region, where research has shown that over half of the football teams founded in the 1876–95 period were named after a neighbourhood or street. Most never progressed beyond local competition and many were short-lived, but it does show the crucial role that local communities played in sustaining the growth and development of football at all levels.

Opposite:
The annual England–Scotland match was one of the most important fixtures in the football calendar. Thousands travelled to Wembley Stadium every two years from Scottish towns and cities to express both community belonging and national pride.

LEAGUE COLOURS

CLAPTON ORIENT

The strength of the bond between club and community is clear in the case of West Ham United. The club emerged from a team of employees at the Thames Ironworks in the East End of London in 1895. Originally created as part of the wider policy of the Ironworks' owner, Arnold Hills, to improve the morale of workers and the reputation of the firm, the club soon outgrew its company roots and in 1900 turned professional and was reborn as West Ham United. Despite limited success, the club soon captured the loyalty of local football fans. A turning-point was its appearance in the 1923 FA Cup final, the first

Above: Clapton Orient was one of the few London clubs to join the mainly Midlands and northern-based Football League before the First World War. It was elected to the League along with Chelsea in 1905.

Right: Community singing was an established part of the FA Cup final experience by the late 1930s. Song sheets were sponsored by national newspapers and distributed to spectators.

A boys' team from Norwich lines up for the camera in the early 1920s. Works' leagues, church leagues and Boys' Brigade and Scouts' leagues were all key facets of recreational football in the inter-war and post-war years.

at Wembley Stadium. West Ham lost the game but thereafter the club became increasingly visible as a representative of the East End and a focal point for civic pride.

Continuity and tradition were hallmarks of the club. There were only four managers and five secretaries in the first seventy-five years of the club's existence, while the board of directors was dominated by two local families – the Cearns and the Pratts – for many years. It established a reputation for promoting from within its ranks and even when players and coaches moved on they often retained a strong identity with West Ham. Teams were also thought traditionally to be built on a nucleus of local talent: players such as centre-half Dick Walker (a one-club professional from 1934 to 1952), born in Hackney, raised in Dagenham and regarded by supporters as the archetypal 'Hammer'. According to the foremost West Ham historian, the club became 'an integral part of the social fabric of the region'.

Hundreds of regional and national publications devoted to football news and gossip appeared before the First World War. *Football Chat* was edited by the Football League President, J. J. Bentley, and focused on the London football scene.

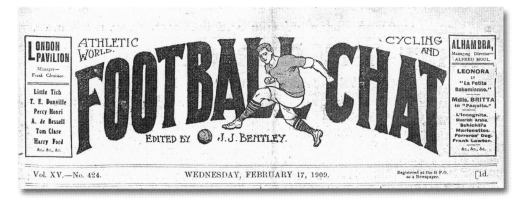

Right: A photo opportunity with the first team squad. The progress of local clubs was covered closely by local newspapers. Journalists and photographers often developed close relationships with the playing staff.

Below: Leicester City supporters at Wembley in 1949. Cup finals were community as well as national events. They boosted the profile of a town or city on the national stage and provided the perfect occasion for a form of popular civic celebration, whatever the result.

The later decades of the twentieth century witnessed an unravelling of the historical weave between football club and community in Britain. Spiralling ticket prices, changing patterns of club ownership and stadium relocations all played their part. The communities themselves changed too. Ethnic minority groups moved into the inner cities where football grounds were generally located while much of the white population moved to the suburbs or beyond. Many clubs struggled to reach out and make links with their increasingly diverse neighbours. When they did so, the initiative often

came from external governmental agencies or the influential Professional Footballers' Association (PFA). This was true of the 'Football in the Community' schemes, which began in the mid-1980s and encouraged clubs to open their facilities to 'community use' and appoint 'community officers'. Some have been rightly criticised for failing to probe beyond the public relations and marketing advantages of such schemes to engage in any meaningful sense with the communities around them.

What constituted a football club's 'community' also became complicated. While clubs always had a wider geographical supporter base than is normally recognised, it is certainly true that fans came from further away to attend matches during the 1990s than in the past. One survey reported that two-thirds of Chelsea season ticket holders in 1998–9 lived outside London. Indeed, many writers increasingly distinguished between local and residential communities, on the one hand, and 'fan' communities on the other. For those who supported from afar, it may be that the relationship was with the club alone and not the local community with which it was originally connected.

Illustrations or photographs of the ground were often used on programme covers. Sheffield Wednesday's Hillsborough was a nationally renowned stadium that regularly staged FA Cup semi-finals, and a source of local pride for at least one half of the city.

Football grounds were often built in the heart of towns and cities. Many were surrounded by houses, with factories, businesses and hospitals close by.

GOING TO THE MATCH

HUNDREDS OF THOUSANDS of people attended professional football matches each week in Britain by the early twentieth century. For many, going to 'the match' was more than a straightforward leisure choice: it was a social habit passed on by family or friends and learnt from an early age. The first visit to a football match could be a formative childhood experience. Parents, older siblings, relatives or family friends commonly introduced youngsters to the game in general, and their club of choice more specifically. Cyril Gibson remembered 'listening in wonderment' as his father and a friend talked about football on the walk to his first Bristol Rovers match at the Eastville Stadium in 1928. Rose Jales recalls being 'drilled' as a child by her father 'about what we were gonna see, the positions of the men, giving me a bit of an idea', before seeing Arsenal play for the first time in the early 1920s. A particular sense of excitement came from being passed down the terraces over the heads of the adult spectators to watch the game close to the pitch.

Football offered a structure and routine to the lives of those who attended. Every other Saturday, spectators would travel by train, tram bus or, if they lived close enough, on foot, to the ground. Some would meet friends or workmates for a drink before the game; some might place a bet or fill in a pools coupon; but others went directly to the ground, many having worked in the morning. There were few amenities at grounds except for drink and food stalls, and little to distract the spectator from the game itself. Local brass bands would play during the half-time break, club programmes informed spectators of the team line-ups and manual scoreboards kept the crowd up-to-date with what was going on at other grounds. But the game's authorities were less keen on other innovations designed to improve the spectator's experience, banning the attachment of numbers to players' shirts before the 1930s and prohibiting floodlit matches until the 1950s.

Much of football's attraction as a spectacle came from the crowd itself. The average football crowd looked fairly uniform before the Second World War. Flat cloth caps predominated in the popular parts of the grounds and

Opposite: fifteen-year-old Luton fan Tony Sendall dressed up in his team's colours and ready for the match against Nottingham Forest in the 1959 cup final.

Supporters brought wooden rattles to football grounds from at least the 1890s. Originally used to scare off birds from fields and in factories to signal the end of shifts, they were adapted, customised and appropriated as part of the culture of football supporting. This one belonged to a Leciester City supporter.

smart casual dress was the norm throughout. There were no replica shirts and, though club colours were increasingly worn, most spectators would consider dressing up only on special occasions such as local 'derbies' or cup finals. But a packed football terrace could be an imposing and fascinating sight, particularly on dark winter afternoons when the lighting of cigarettes and pipes at half-time resembled 'an illumination' or 'a monstrous Christmas tree'.

Football grounds were always extremely noisy places. The cheering of a partisan crowd could be an intimidating experience for players. The England captain Billy Wright recalled his first experience of the notorious 'roar' associated with Glasgow's Hampden Park in 1946: 'It was as if the heavens had opened. There was a

A group of dedicated Middlesbrough supporters known as the 'Ayresome Angels' who followed the club home and away from the 1960s. *Football League Review* described them as 'the best behaved bunch of lads and lassies in modern football'.

gigantic roar, resembling the kind I believe precedes an earthquake. My ear drums felt shattered. The turf beneath my boots literally shook.'

Singing and chanting added to the atmosphere of the occasion. Spectators adopted, and sometimes adapted, the popular songs of the time, from the Edwardian music hall to the pop music of the 1960s and 1970s. Harry Lauder's 'I Love a Lassie', for example, was heard on a number of Football League grounds in 1911. Many clubs developed their own identifiable songs.

Left: Between 1895 and 1914 the FA Cup final was played at Crystal Palace. Attendances were often estimated at over 70,000 or 80,000 in the decade before the First World War.

Below: 'Away' supporters at an FA Cup tie in the 1920s. Fans were prepared to travel in significant numbers to support their club in important games.

A record crowd of 47,298 watching Leicester City play Tottenham Hotspur in 1928. Thousands of spectators were locked outside the ground and some risked serious injury to get a view of the match.

Norwich's 'On the Ball City' is said to date from the very foundation of the club in 1902. Portsmouth's 'Pompey Chimes', Newcastle United's 'Blaydon Races' and West Ham's 'I'm Forever Blowing Bubbles' were all sung during the 1930s, if not before. Liverpool fans on the 'Kop' terrace at Anfield during the 1960s were responsible for popularising a number of generic football songs but became particularly famous for their versions of Beatles songs as well as their stirring rendition of 'You'll Never Walk Alone'. Here as elsewhere, songs and chants were invented for every player and for most occasions. The performances of the terrace choirs became an essential part of the spectacle: indeed some people 'went to see the Kop sing as much as watch the players play'.

A Mass-Observation report of a match at Bolton Wanderers during the late 1930s offered a rare anthropological insight into the behaviour and sub-culture of the football crowd. As well as noting the comments of the supporters ('If only they'd kick it, it might just deflect off somebody', 'Knock him over', 'What a bloody shot', and so on), the observer analysed their actions, body language and behaviour in relation to one another and the players. He commented on the 'vindictive nature' of the crowd ('all tell the players what should have been done'), but recognised the complex emotional journey that supporters went through: 'All ideas and feelings … rapidly changing – up comes fury, exaltation, sarcasm.' His main conclusion was a revealing assessment of football's appeal for the inter-war British male: 'The only place men can shout is here and only place where they can be really free. So do shout. Can't at home or at work [sic].' The notion of football as an emotional release or an escape from the realities of everyday life was

Left: A Chelsea match programme from the beginning of the Second World War. Organised football continued throughout the war on an ad-hoc basis. The government recognised its value in boosting morale among servicemen and civilians.

Below: Tickets to Wembley matches included a plan of the stadium with the location of turnstiles. Many spectators arrived early at cup finals and international matches to chant, sing and generally soak up the atmosphere of the occasion.

common across time and place. 'You lose all your worries', was one view of the fan experience of the 1960s, 'and for two hours that's all that matters. Everything outside is irrelevant.'

For much of the twentieth century, conditions at British football grounds were extremely poor. Little attention was paid to the comfort of spectators. The cheaper ticket holders often

Goalmouth action from an FA Cup tie in 1949. League crowds reached a post-war peak of 41.2 million during this season. Many ground attendance records were set around this time.

The kick-off of a match involving Everton in the 1920s. Watching football was recognised by the political establishment as a pillar of working-class cultural life between the wars.

stood on raised banks of earth, which could become muddy very quickly in wet weather. Concrete terracing had been pioneered at Bradford City and Sunderland before the First World War, and for the new Wembley Stadium built in 1923, but it was expensive and became widespread only from the 1940s. The covering of the terraces took longer still in many cases, leaving standing spectators exposed to the elements. Overcrowding was common on the big occasions and a good view of the game was rare. Writing in 1937, one

journalist thought it 'impudent' that the Arsenal directors should 'ask the man who pays to turn himself into a sardine'. Some fans simply walked out when it became clear they would be unable to see any of the action; others got a better view by climbing on to stanchions and stand roofs.

Spectators were well aware of the potential dangers of going to a football match. Fainting was a regular occurrence, the usual practice being that bodies were passed over the heads of the crowd to be treated by the ambulance men below. The authorities recognised that the over-packing of the terraces and the swaying of the crowd could lead to crushing, and possible injury and death. The warnings had been there since 1923, when over a thousand spectators were injured at the first Wembley FA Cup final, and were underlined in 1934, when a Sheffield Wednesday supporter died as a result of being crushed against railings. In March 1946, thirty-three fans were killed in a crush following the closure of turnstiles at an FA Cup tie between Bolton Wanderers and Stoke City. A Home Office inquiry into the disaster recommended that all football grounds should be licensed by local authorities. Nothing was done. Pressure at the local level sometimes forced change. In 1935 the Chief Constable of Norwich had deemed the City club's dilapidated ground, The Nest, to be 'dangerous to spectators' and persuaded the directors to construct a safer and more modern stadium at Carrow Road. But it took another disaster, at Ibrox Park in Glasgow in 1971, where sixty-

Photograph of Norwich City's ground, The Nest, from the mid-1930s. The ground was considered ill-equipped to handle the large crowds the club attracted after promotion to the Second Division of the Football League in 1934.

The installation of floodlighting (in this case at Leicester City's Filbert Street) made football games in the evening a regular feature of British football culture. Evening matches against foreign teams, often televised, were particularly popular in the 1950s.

The opinion of the professional game's administering body was communicated to supporters through the *Football League Review*. A lively and often controversial read, it came free with club programmes in the 1960s and 1970s.

six spectators were crushed to death leaving the ground, for a system of local control and licensing to be finally set up, under the terms of the 1975 Safety of Sports Grounds Act.

Hooliganism was another unsavoury element of the match day experience. Crowd unrest had existed almost from the beginnings of the professional game but in the 1960s and 1970s there was a significant increase in incidents and a new phenomenon of organised fighting between rival groups of young men inside and outside grounds. Between August 1970 and October 1976, the FA dealt with 129 incidents of hooliganism, ranging from the throwing of missiles at players and officials to pitch invasions.

One of the most serious incidents took place in March 1974. Newcastle United were losing at home to Second Division Nottingham Forest when United supporters ran on to the pitch, forcing the game to be delayed. 'Thousands of them have invaded the field', BBC radio commentator Bill Bothwell told his listeners. 'Never before have I seen a situation, or a scene, on any English football ground, quite like this.' Bothwell exaggerated the numbers involved but a Forest fan later recalled being frightened at a football match for the only time in his life. The response of the football authorities was remarkably tame. The FA ordered the match to be replayed (Newcastle had eventually won 4-3) and banned Newcastle from playing at home in the competition the following year. That was all. For barrister Edward Grayson, this was 'the green light to hooliganism'. Yet hooliganism was never entirely a football problem: its causes were complex and varied. Media references to 'animals', 'yobs' and 'thugs' were counterproductive, allowing the government to ignore for too long its responsibility for a problem that had deep social roots.

Although all sorts of people attended matches, the football crowd was never a perfect cross-section of British society. For seventy or eighty years from the 1890s, it was dominated by the working class, particularly the skilled and better-paid strata who could afford to attend regularly. Middle-class spectatorship was more widespread than is often assumed but the more affluent often watched in a different context: from the stands rather than the terraces, and in greater numbers on special occasions, such as cup ties. Women went to football from the start but they were always in the minority. Descriptions and photographs demonstrate that football crowds were predominantly male. They were also overwhelmingly white. The increased proportion of black footballers on the pitch from the 1970s was never replicated in the crowd. Clubs based in multicultural parts of London and other big cities did manage to develop pockets of black and Asian support over time but the frequency of racial abuse on the terraces meant that football grounds were a generally unwelcoming and hostile environment for ethnic minorities for most of the twentieth century.

An aerial photograph of Goodison Park in 1987. As in many cases, residential housing had developed around the ground and the club remained physically at the centre of the local neighbourhood.

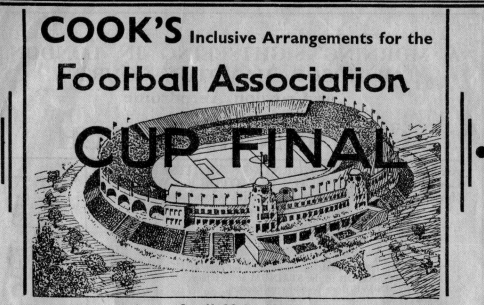

THE BUSINESS OF FOOTBALL

'To be successful', wrote the former Football League president and Manchester United secretary J. J. Bentley in 1911, 'football must be worked on business lines, for in many instances the annual turnover of clubs exceeds £20,000 per annum, and to deal with such large sums necessitates the introduction of business principles'. This did not equate with 'commercialism' in Bentley's view, however, a very different principle against which 'a strong line must be drawn'. Over half a century later, a government report on football came to a similar conclusion:

> League football is not a 'commercial' operation in the same sense that a manufacturing or service industry is commercial; but it is subject to financial pressures like any other entertainment business. If its income does not meet its expenditure then, in the short run, it is in difficulties, and in the long run it will either have to reduce its level of operations or go out of business altogether.

Both authorities acknowledged that football was indeed a business but of a peculiar kind, in which points, cups and championships mattered more than profits.

The first football clubs were run by voluntary committees drawn from the broader membership. With the arrival of professionalism in 1885, costs soon increased and most ambitious clubs chose to adopt limited liability status over the next two decades. A number of restrictions existed, however, to limit the possible financial returns that could be made from the sport. Directors were not paid and shareholders' dividends in England were limited, to 5 per cent before 1914 and 7.5 per cent from then onwards. No such restrictions existed in Scotland but only the two biggest clubs – Celtic and Rangers – ever paid significant sums out to shareholders or directors.

Everton was considered the wealthiest club in England before the First World War, recording a surplus every year bar one from 1891 to 1914, but most of its rivals were existing from hand to mouth. The finances of many

Opposite: Thomas Cook began organising excursions to international matches and cup finals in the 1890s. In some communities, supporters joined special savings clubs to help fund their trips.

professional clubs were precarious for the first few decades of professionalism. A considerable proportion simply went bust and others, such as West Bromwich Albion in the years 1905–8, teetered on the brink of bankruptcy, surviving only through special fund-raising and appeals to its creditors. Potential speculators, *The Times* noted in 1910, could see that more clubs 'were in pecuniary difficulties than ever before' and that football 'is not really a money-making business'.

The significance of the finances of the 'national game' was acknowledged by the appearance of an article in the *Economist* in April 1937. It estimated average gate receipts for First Division clubs to be £1,500 'on fine afternoons', which equated to seasonal takings of £640,000 in the top division and £1,500,000 annually in the whole of the four-division Football League. Against this, clubs paid out on wages, benefits, transfer fees, ground expenses, shareholders' dividends and debt repayment. Spending large

Right: Even in the 1920s, a large proportion of club expenditure was devoted to players' wages, benefits and transfer fees.

Below: Postcards featuring football-related cartoons, photographs and illustrations were popular in the early decades of the professional game.

amounts on buying in players, in particular, was highly risky, illustrated by the £40,000 Aston Villa unsuccessfully paid out on seven new players during the 1935–6 season to avoid relegation. Football, the article concluded, was 'not a game in which large fortunes are directly made. Players, shareholders and directors earn only a modest reward, and take a good deal of risk.'

For many years, shareholders and directors invested in football hoping for emotional and social returns rather than financial ones. Many shareholders were fans whose small investment was just another way of demonstrating their commitment to the club. Profit was not a motive. Directors were likewise more interested in playing success than in making money. Any profits that were made were generally used to improve the ground or strengthen the squad. Directors were typically local businessmen who looked on their involvement as a civic duty.

A trading card featuring the Everton badge and colours from the 1930s. A variety of firms, from tea manufacturers to publishers of boys' comics, issued cards of clubs and footballers in an attempt to boost sales.

Bradford Park Avenue was one of a handful of clubs that went out of business before the 1990s. The club was voted out of the Football League in 1970 and went into liquidation soon after.

BRADFORD P.A. F.C.
Division Four 1968-1969

Back Row:—Graham Tanner ☐ Gary Hudson ☐ Glen Andrews ☐ Gary Halliday ☐ John Hardie
David Lawson ☐ Tommy Singleton ☐ Tony Harris ☐ Steve Gibson ☐ Phil Robinson
Front Row:—Stuart Darfield ☐ John Sykes (now with Wrexham) ☐ Keith Cockburn (now with Grimsby Town)
Derek Draper (now with Chester) ☐ Mike Walker ☐ Geoff Gould ☐ John Clancy

Stanley Waddilove of Bradford Park Avenue was a classic example. From a wealthy Methodist family that owned a large clothing and supply company, Waddilove joined the Park Avenue board in 1923 and later become its director until 1955. A domineering figure he may have been but his financial commitment to the club over these years was considerable. He was said to have regarded the club as his 'life's hobby'.

FA restrictions did not prevent the involvement in football of businessmen who had more speculative motives. An early example was Henry Norris. A property developer, Mayor of Fulham and chairman of Fulham FC, Norris took over the struggling Second Division side Woolwich Arsenal in 1910. Three years later, he moved Arsenal across the Thames to Highbury in north London, where there was a larger potential audience than in Woolwich. More audacious still was the tactical manoeuvring and lobbying that got Arsenal elected to the First Division of the Football League in 1919 despite finishing only fifth in the Second Division in the 1914–15 season. Described as 'a thin autocrat with a walrus moustache' who 'welcomed neither criticism nor advice', Norris was a powerful but unpopular figure in the football politics of the day. He was in some respects an early prototype of the more commercially driven, entrepreneurial directors of the late twentieth century. In 1927 he was found guilty of receiving payment from

John Player's 'Hints on Association Football' series highlighted technical aspects of passing, shooting, heading and so on. The tackle and the shoulder charge were elements of the game at which the British considered themselves particularly skilled.

SHOOTING ON THE RUN. Although some players can kick a dead ball successfully, the best shooting chance is with a moving ball which gives additional power. The ball should be driven with the instep (that is with the toe pointing to the ground) and the player should be over the ball with the non-kicking foot well forward. If the player is too far behind the ball, it will be likely to rise and thus travel over the goal. After having chosen the place to aim at, keep your eye on the ball. (No. 34.)

THE TACKLE. The secret of a successful tackle lies in judging precisely the moment when one should go forward in the attempt to secure the ball. Sometimes it is necessary to stand off and wait for the opportunity to occur ; to dash in when the opponent has the ball under close control is to play into his hands. The best chance is to make the challenge before the man has been able to collect the ball and bring it to his feet. If the ball cannot be retrieved, your aim should be to compel the man to part with it, and to cover him so that he can only do this in one way. (No. 35.)

THE SHOULDER CHARGE. Although the shoulder charge is not used to-day as much as formerly, it is still permitted by the rules and may sometimes be introduced with excellent results. But to be fair, the charge must be with the shoulder and not a push with the elbow, and care should be taken to avoid striking the opponent in the back. The proper use of the charge is to knock a man off the ball, and so permit it to be taken from him ; if a charge can be made when he has one foot off the ground it is almost certain to be successful. (No. 36.)

Arsenal for a chauffeur and a new car. The FA banned him from football for life.

By the 1960s, there was considerable disquiet about the finances of football and the way clubs were run. Political and Economic Planning's 1966 report demonstrated that the gap

ITV...

FOR THE BEST IN LEAGUE SOCCER

ITV INDEPENDENT TELEVISION

Above: Commercial television companies included football in their schedules from their arrival in 1955. Programmes consisting of the highlights of weekend league fixtures were the staple of regional television companies in the 1960s and 1970s.

£500 for TEN FOOTER FORECASTS! NOW TH

THE FOOTBALL AN SPOR FAVOURIT

2D

REGGIE RUFFLES FOOTBALLER DETECTIVE

Meet him Inside!

Left: Football magazines and comics often featured a one-off football story or a serial as well as profiles of leading teams and players. Many were aimed specifically at boys or the adolescent market.

between rich and poor was big and growing. Many of the smaller clubs could survive only through the sizeable contributions of supporters' clubs and redistribution across the league of gate income and other sources. Directors were considered out of touch with supporters and players and insufficiently tuned in to modern management and marketing techniques. A 1964 survey revealed that the average age of directors was fifty-eight and that 38 per cent were over the age of sixty. According to Peter Douglas, a public relations consultant who worked for Crystal Palace at the end of the 1960s, what was lacking in boardrooms was 'expertise in financial and administrative areas, skill in personnel management and a knowledge of basic public relations'.

The football authorities had traditionally kept their distance from the pools industry and television, areas in which critics saw considerable financial opportunities. Moral objections to gambling among Football League officials meant that a proposed financial deal in the 1930s with the Pools Promoters' Association (PPA) collapsed. By 1964, the PPA had agreed to give 1 per cent of its gross earnings (with a guaranteed minimum of £40,000) to football. This provided crucial income for smaller clubs but was nowhere near as lucrative as similar deals in other parts of Europe. Radio and television coverage was initially opposed and then only grudgingly accepted by football's leaders during the post-war years. As a result, early contracts yielded modest sums until 1978, when a new four-year £9.2 million deal was negotiated by the Football League. A new contract for live Football League matches followed in 1983. The game's dependence on television revenue was now firmly established.

Below right: Tommy Lawton's *Football Is My Business* was one of the first post-war football autobiographies. Published in 1946, when Lawton was still only twenty-seven, it included stories of his career with club and country and his wartime experiences.

Far right: The publication of ghosted autobiographies of star footballers increased markedly in the 1950s. Most were fairly anodyne but a new trend for the memoirs of outspoken, controversial characters such as Scottish international Tommy Docherty developed in the 1960s and 1970s.

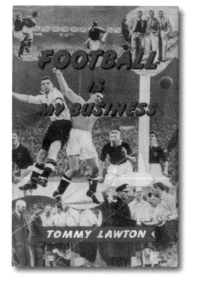

A set of cigarette cards from the 1930s. Firms such as Wills, Players, Churchmans and Carreras produced thousands of football-related cigarette cards in Britain before the Second World War.

If football itself was a business, there was a raft of ancillary industries that grew up around it. Manufacturers and retailers supplied balls, boots, shirts, shorts and socks; engineers and builders designed and constructed turnstiles, pavilions and grandstands; restaurants, caterers and publicans offered the spectator food and drink before, during and after the match. A range of companies used football to sell their products. From the late 1890s, cigarette companies produced thousands of cards featuring football players and teams. Potions and liniments aimed at the recreational athlete were endorsed by footballers. For West Ham's trainer Chas Paynter it was Sanitas Embrocation, while Liverpool's Tom Bromilow swore by 'Phosferine – The

Greatest of All Tonics'. It is impossible to know how much Arsenal, the First Division champions in 1930–1, were paid for wearing and advertising Bukta outfits ('Shorts tailored to fit smartly over the hips, loose around the seat and legs'). But we know that Stanley Matthews received £20 per week for wearing Co-op football boots in 1951. By the 1980s, Bryan Robson could sign a boot endorsement contract of £25,000 a year. Kevin Keegan had agreements with a range of companies selling sports goods, toiletries, designer suits, breakfast cereals and baked beans.

Members of the victorious England World Cup team were much in demand to endorse products in the late 1960s and 1970s. As one of the world's best goalkeepers, Gordon Banks was associated with success and reliability.

Local firms had been advertising their products at grounds and in club programmes for many years. From the 1960s, it also became possible to sponsor match balls or an individual player's strip. Sponsorship of competitions or on team shirts was resisted by the governing bodies, who remained concerned that it would lead to unbridled commercialisation. When non-league Kettering Town arranged for a local tyre company to place its name on the shirt in 1976, it was disciplined by the FA. Derby County brokered a sponsorship deal with Saab in 1977 that guaranteed it £100,000 (including a car for each first-team player) in return for ground advertising and re-naming the main stand, but the club would apparently have received double had shirt advertising been allowed. The ban was lifted soon after and the authorities finally relented on competition sponsors. The League Cup became the Milk Cup in 1982 and the Football League was the Canon League from 1983.

The Manchester-based sports clothing firm Umbro was a regular supplier of kits for football and rugby teams. In 1934, both FA Cup finalists, Manchester City and Portsmouth, wore Umbro kit, and in 1954 the company began a long association with the England national team.

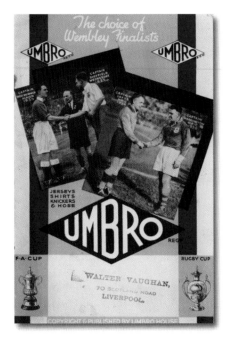

The business of football was changing. The ceiling on shareholders' dividends and the ban on the payment of directors were lifted. Gate revenues were no longer shared and television money was less equally distributed. A new breed of club director came into the game from the finance, advertising, property development and newspaper industries. New avenues for increasing revenue were explored. Company mergers between bitter sporting rivals were considered. The link between football and business, always present, was more visible than ever before.

The connections between tobacco companies and football continued into the post-war era. *The Park Drive Book of Football*, advertised here in the late 1960s, was one of a number of publications catering for followers of the game.

BRITAIN VERSUS THE WORLD

F OOTBALL'S global diffusion was a complex and uneven process. On one level, it involved the straightforward movement of people. British sailors, soldiers, administrators, teachers, students and engineers carried an interest in, and knowledge of, the game with them as they travelled around the world from the late nineteenth century. If they stayed long enough, they might set up a club. In Italy, some of the best known teams, such as AC Milan and Genoa, started life as combined 'cricket and football clubs' for the expatriate British community.

Elsewhere, particular individuals were instrumental in the popularisation of football. In Buenos Aires, a Scottish teacher, Alexander Watson Hutton, started his own English High School in 1884, placing considerable emphasis on physical education, and football in particular. He founded the Argentine Association Football League in 1893 with five clubs consisting of mainly British players. But the popularity of football quickly spread beyond the British community. By 1903, there were four divisions and the rules and meetings were held in Spanish rather than English. Charles Miller was the key figure in Brazil. Born in Brazil, he was schooled in England, where he learnt football, and returned to organise the game through the influential São Paulo Athletic Club.

It was by no means inevitable, of course, that a passion for football would be transferred from the British to the locals. Those who witnessed the earliest displays in their home land may well have been mesmerised by the strange sight of foreigners in shorts knocking a ball around with their feet. They may have wanted to play themselves. It was certainly a relatively simple game to learn and little equipment was needed.

ITINERARY

**EVERTON
FOOTBALL CLUB**

❧

**TOUR IN GERMANY
1932**

❧

Matches at

DRESDEN	-	May 14th
BRESLAU	-	May 16th
BERLIN -	-	May 21st
HANOVER	-	May 22nd
NURNBERG	-	May 26th
COLOGNE	-	May 29th

The British themselves played a crucial role but football also benefited from a prevailing mood of anglophilia in parts of Europe and beyond. To members of the internationally minded continental bourgeoisie, Britain was the epitome of modernity and innovation. Many visited Britain as students or met those who had done so in schools and technical colleges on the continent. Playing football was a point of connection and a symbol of modernity for these young, ambitious, cosmopolitan men. One was Vittorio Pozzo, an Italian who studied commerce and languages in Switzerland, England and Germany before returning home and becoming a member of Torino Football Club. He later became a renowned sports journalist and manager of the Italian national side that won the World Cup in 1934 and 1938. Others travelled across borders and continents to establish careers and, in their spare time, to found football clubs and organise competitions.

Not everyone fell easily for the charms of the so-called people's game. In the territories of the formal Empire, it was cricket and rugby rather than football that took the eye of the local population. In the United States, baseball had already established itself as the popular sport of the urban working classes by the 1860s. Football became popular in the industrial cities of the north-east and in St Louis and Chicago but it remained a marginal sport associated with foreigners and outsiders. English sports such as football were popular among the German middle class but were criticised by nationalist leaders who favoured indigenous forms of gymnastics. Football was condemned as an unwanted alien import and an uncivilised and unsophisticated pastime. Its 'most characteristic physical motion', according to one critic, 'resembled kicking the dog'. In 1910, the German football federation was still small compared to its gymnastics rival (82,000 as against one million members) but over time it grew in

The awarding of caps by the British football associations for international appearances dates back to the 1870s, when amateur footballers wore caps when playing. England players received a small match fee but selection was considered an honour for player and club.

Arsenal was the most successful English team of the inter-war years. Under managers Herbert Chapman and George Allison, the club won five First Division championships and two FA Cups. It was also one of the more frequent professional touring teams.

THEY GO BY COOKS

Personality Parade

A T the head of the Football League's First Division as the 1953-54 season closes are Wolverhampton Wanderers, who won their last game of the season against the Spurs on April 24th.

Here they are just boarding their S.A.S. DC6 Cloudmaster, bound for Scandinavia.

Sydney Head, Sales Manager of S.A.S., is the second man from the left, with, on his right, A. Furby, Air Travel Department, who had the bright idea of sending us the picture.

Names of the players are:
From top, Peter Broadbent, C. Hunter (Director) wearing glasses, Tommy McDonald (left) Ron Flowers (striped tie), Bill Guttridge with hand on Les Smith's shoulder. At left again is Ron Stockin, Roy Pritchard's wavy hair stays put while Noel Dwyer's blows about. Roy Swinbourne (wearing blazer) is behind Norman Deeley, Eddie Stuart is next below, and Bob Mason on his right. At the foot of the stairs are Bill Shorthouse (carrying coat), Manager Stan Cullis (wearing a hat), once England's captain, Colin Booth with all the curly hair, trainer Joe Gardiner, Eddie Clamp, J. Marshall (Director), with hat and glasses, and John Timmins on the extreme right. Wolves' skipper, Billy Wright, had a date in Budapest when this was taken.

Why not send us a note of the famous people who book with you?

This article on Wolverhampton Wanderers' tour to Scandinavia in 1954 appeared in the Thomas Cook magazine. Wolves had played a number of high-profile games against Soviet and Hungarian teams in previous seasons that drew big gates and large television audiences.

popularity among the industrial workers of areas such as the Ruhr Valley.

British touring teams were instrumental in popularising the game in new territories. The first tourists were amateur clubs who regarded themselves as 'football missionaries'. The Corinthians were one example, visiting South Africa (twice), Brazil (three times) and the United States and Canada all before the First World War. The Middlesex Wanderers, with no regular home ground or fixtures, existed solely for the purpose of touring. More remarkable still was the story of the Islington Corinthians, a team comprising mainly students, teachers and clerks that competed no higher than the North London Thursday League but nonetheless undertook its own world tour between October 1937 and June 1938. The party travelled 35,000 miles and played ninety-five games, beginning in the Netherlands, and taking in Switzerland, Egypt, India, Burma, Malaya, Singapore, the Dutch East Indies, Hong Kong, the Philippines, China, Japan, the United States and Canada.

Touring could be financially lucrative, as professional clubs soon began to recognise. Vienna had been the destination of choice before 1914 but thereafter offers arrived annually from all parts of Europe and North and South America. Not all trips were the relaxing holidays that players hoped for. During a match at the Boca Juniors ground in Buenos Aires in 1929, the Chelsea team was pelted with oranges, assaulted by its Argentine opponents and had the tyres of its charabanc slashed. Some touring teams did themselves few favours. Indifferent displays and poor behaviour by Newcastle United players during a central European tour the same year led the Hungarian FA to cancel its contract with the club. The press thought that these football 'joy-rides' were damaging for British prestige abroad. Some players admitted that they would have preferred to be with their families or playing golf and cricket in the summer. Yet the experience of touring had its wider benefits. It broadened the cultural and culinary, if not always the linguistic, horizons of the young working-class men who made up the bulk of football's workforce. A number of players' autobiographies referred to the 'travelling education' that came with being a professional. 'Had it not been for football', wrote Raich Carter in 1950, 'I should never have left England.'

The British influence on world football was also evident in the hundreds of coaches who travelled and worked abroad. The increasing popularity of football in continental Europe from the 1920s onwards was frequently credited to 'the systematic training of young players by old British professionals'. The most successful was Jimmy Hogan, a former inside-forward with Bolton Wanderers, who moved to the

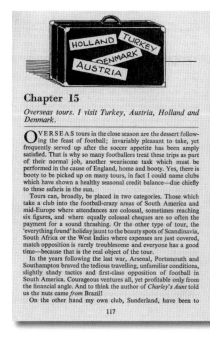

Chapter 15

Overseas tours. I visit Turkey, Austria, Holland and Denmark.

OVERSEAS tours in the close season are the dessert following the feast of football; invariably pleasant to take, yet frequently served up after the soccer appetite has been amply satisfied. That is why so many footballers treat these trips as part of their normal job, another wearisome task which must be performed in the cause of England, home and booty. Yes, there is booty to be picked up on many tours, in fact I could name clubs which have shown a healthy seasonal credit balance—due chiefly to these safaris in the sun.

Tours can, broadly, be placed in two categories. Those which take a club into the football-crazy areas of South America and mid-Europe where attendances are colossal, sometimes reaching six figures, and where equally colossal cheques are so often the payment for a sound thrashing. Or the other type of tour, the 'everything found' holiday jaunt to the beauty spots of Scandinavia, South Africa or the West Indies where expenses are just covered, match opposition is rarely troublesome and everyone has a good time—because that is the real object of the tour.

In the years following the last war, Arsenal, Portsmouth and Southampton braved the tedious travelling, unfamiliar conditions, slightly shady tactics and first-class opposition of football in South America. Courageous ventures all, yet profitable only from the financial angle. And to think the author of *Charley's Aunt* told us the nuts came *from* Brazil!

On the other hand my own club, Sunderland, have been to

117

Foreign tours and experiences abroad began to form an important part of footballers' autobiographies in the 1950s and 1960s. This chapter is from Len Shackleton's *Clown Prince of Soccer*, published in 1955.

PRAGUE 1934. ENGLISH TEAM.

After his first international in April, 1934, against Scotland at Wembley, the author was selected for the England tour of Hungary and Czechoslovakia. Here is an autographed photograph of the England party which lost to both Hungary and Czechoslovakia by two goals to one.

An autographed photograph of the England squad that toured Hungary and Czechoslovakia in May 1934. Central European teams presented the stiffest opposition to British sides at the time. England lost 2-1 in both Budapest and Prague.

Netherlands as national coach in 1911 and went on to become one of Europe's most sought-after coaches over the next three decades. Another relatively modest player, George Raynor coached Sweden to Olympic success in 1948 and second place to the Brazilians in the 1958 World Cup. By the 1970s, British coaches were in demand in every part of the world and particularly in 'developing' football regions such as North America and the Middle East.

Gary Lineker playing for Tottenham Hotspur in 1989. Lineker was one of a small number of leading British footballers who joined foreign clubs (in his case in Spain and Japan) during the 1980s and 1990s.

British referees were also admired for their quality and scrupulous honesty. They were also independent, which was important to the Argentinian FA when they recruited a number of British officials to take charge of the bulk of First Division matches between 1948 and 1954. By the 1950s, British referees could be found throughout South America. One, Jack Barrack from Northampton, became the top referee in Brazil and controlled twelve out of the twenty-nine matches at the South American Championship of 1949. The British were widely considered the best referees in the world at the time. At the 1950 World Cup in Brazil, ten of the twenty-two games were entrusted to British referees.

There is, however, another side to Britain's relationship with world football. For many years, the British football authorities took up a stance of indifference and arrogant superiority about the progress of the game beyond its shores. They joined FIFA, the world governing body, late and spent most of the period before 1945 outside its orbit. They refused to take part in the first three World Cups and did not take those they entered particularly seriously until the 1960s. The Football League was particularly slow to recognise the importance of European club competition in the 1950s, regarding it initially as little more than a distraction from the regular business of domestic football.

In truth, the British regarded themselves as pre-eminent among football nations long after they had been caught up and eclipsed by their rivals on the field. Even after the England team had suffered humiliating home and away defeats against Hungary in 1953–4, the authorities were slow to adapt their ideologies and structures. Journalists, managers and players acknowledged that the British were no longer world leaders in the game. The difference was clear to many. As the president of the Hungarian FA put it: 'what you played was industry and what we played was art.' But football based on power and pace continued to overshadow technique and skill. Coaching remained secondary to natural talent and instinct. The long and gruelling domestic season was what mattered most. International football lagged some way behind.

England's 1966 World Cup victory was a triumph for the team and its coach, Alf Ramsey. Some saw it as a vindication of the established English/British way of doing things. But it did little to improve the image of English football abroad. The next tournament, in Mexico, was a public relations disaster for the England team. In a confidential

The teams for one of the games on the Moscow Dynamo tour of Britain in 1945. The Soviet side beat Arsenal 4-3. Stanley Matthews, a guest player for Arsenal, rated them 'the finest team to have visited this island'.

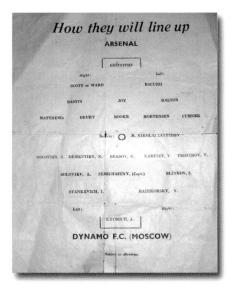

55

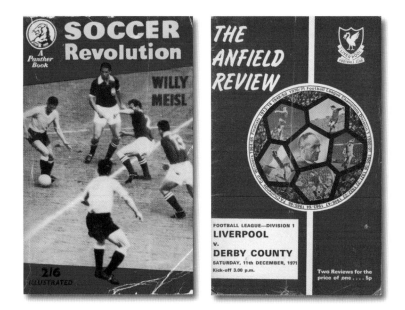

Right: The Austrian journalist Willy Meisl's *Soccer Revolution*, first published in 1955, was a powerful critique of the English style of football. According to Meisl, the English game was a 'safety first' approach built on 'destructive, defensive, spoiling tactics'.

Far right: A Liverpool match programme from the early 1970s. Liverpool was to become the most successful English team of all time over the next two decades, winning eleven League championships and four European Cups between 1972–3 and 1989–90.

Opposite: Kevin Keegan pictured playing for England against Northern Ireland's John O'Neill. Matches between the British national teams were the main 'international' fixtures in the football calendar for many years. But the 'Home Internationals' declined in significance during the 1970s and 1980s.

report, the FA identified hostility from the Mexicans as 'the most disturbing feature' of the competition. There had been 'downright open antagonism' to the England players and supporters, who were jeered and abused throughout. The British ambassador to Mexico City was moved to write to the Foreign Office about the hostility, which he put down to a combination of recent sporting tensions, 'Mexican chauvinism' and poor public relations between the England party and the press. Back in London, it was accepted that the English were culpable for some of the problems and 'that we [the FA] have damaged our own reputation and the name of the UK'.

By the 1970s, the British nations were performing modestly, at best, on the field. England failed to qualify for the World Cup finals of 1974 and 1978 and neither Northern Ireland nor Wales had played in one since 1958. The Scottish were more successful but failed to progress from their group in Argentina '78, a tournament that some thought they could win. British influence in the committee rooms of European and world football had also declined. Stanley Rous's reign as FIFA president ended in 1974 and there was no British administrator of equivalent international standing to take his place. British representatives expressed disquiet at the changing politics of world football and, in particular, the rise in influence of African and Asian nations. Behind the scenes, consideration was even given to the possibility of withdrawing from FIFA again. For far too long, the British struggled to come to terms with the fact that 'their' game had become a genuinely global passion.

Nat Lofthouse, the Bolton and England centre forward has two Chelsea men to deal with, Stan Willemse and Ron Greenwood (who is now with Fulham), but he rises above both to make a fine header.

FOOTBALL REMADE

BRITISH FOOTBALL changed forever on 15 April 1989. Ninety-six Liverpool supporters died that day at the beginning of an FA Cup semi-final tie at Hillsborough stadium in Sheffield. The tragedy was the result of poor decisions on the day but also of years of limited investment in facilities and a disregard for the treatment of spectators. The subsequent inquiry, conducted by Lord Justice Taylor, concluded that a new attitude to crowd safety and the club–fan relationship was needed. With football's voluntary governing bodies unable to put their own houses in order, government intervention was needed. All grounds in the top two divisions of the Football League in England and the Scottish Premier Division were required to become all-seated by the beginning of the 1994–5 season. Perimeter fencing was to be removed and a new system of inspection and regulation of grounds put into place. Moreover, the Taylor Report of 1990 called for a more enlightened and responsible attitude to the grass-roots supporter. Football needed to be modernised and the interests of fans could no longer be disregarded, or their support taken for granted.

In the two decades following the Hillsborough disaster and the Taylor Report, the landscape of British football changed almost beyond recognition. The grounds themselves were either transformed through redevelopment or sold off and the club relocated. Between 1988 and 2007, nearly a quarter of the 102 clubs who played in England's top four divisions moved location. Old and decrepit grounds were replaced by modern stadiums with improved facilities and multi-purpose uses that included bowling alleys, conference centres, multiplex cinemas, even hotels. Changing perspectives were often reflected in stadium names, with sponsors (Reebok Stadium at Bolton, Britannia Stadium in Stoke and Emirates Stadium at Arsenal) and club chairmen (Madejski Stadium in Reading and the Kassam Stadium in Oxford) prominent. Critics bemoaned the lack of atmosphere in these production-line venues but there was to be no going back to the days of terracing.

Supporters, too, seemed to have changed. The profile of football fans became more socially diverse during the 1990s, with many clubs acquiring

Opposite:
An illustration of Nat Lofthouse rising for a header during the 1950s. Lofthouse spent his entire career with Bolton Wanderers, his home-town club. He remained a symbol of club and town up to, and beyond, his death in January 2011.

Independent fanzines produced by supporters and sold outside grounds were an important feature of football culture from the late 1980s.

Known by devotees as the 'Theatre of Dreams', Manchester United's Old Trafford was one of the most iconic of British football stadiums. The addition of extra tiers on two stands in 2006 took the capacity to 76,212.

a more middle-class, female and family audience. The downside of these changes was that traditional working-class fans felt that they were being squeezed out by excessive ticket prices. 'Bank managers and stuff go now', complained a Newcastle United fan in 1998. 'There's not many normal people, working-class people with kids, who've got four hundred pound to splash out on a season ticket.' Supporters were now encouraged to spend more and more on replica shirts and other club merchandise. Their relationship with the clubs was increasingly as customers rather than supporters. This led to a feeling of alienation among those fans whose main connection with 'their' team was now through satellite television and the club shop.

The engine for football's transformation was the Premier League, founded in 1992. Initially created by the FA and the leading English clubs

to increase television and sponsorship revenues *and* to improve the fortunes of the England team, the latter was very quickly jettisoned at the expense of the former. Major contracts with satellite television companies underpinned the commercial expansion of the League and its clubs during the 1990s. With no regulation or ceiling on salaries, English clubs were able to attract the very best players from across the world. Football was more newsworthy than ever and footballers were transformed into popular cultural icons and celebrities. The Premier League, moreover, became a global brand, watched by millions of people in almost every part of the world. It also increasingly attracted wealthy foreign owners, whose presence generated concern and sometimes virulent hostility among supporters.

For all that the 1990s and early twenty-first century witnessed a remaking of British football, links with the past remained important. In an age of foreign players and ground relocations, interest in the history and heritage of the game blossomed. Stands were named after former players and managers and statues and sculptures of earlier stars were commissioned.

New cultures of football supporting developed in the 1990s. These were characterised by an increase of colour, raucous behaviour and a carnival atmosphere, influenced in part by the followers of continental teams.

A magazine dedicated to Scottish junior football dating from the early 1990s. Semi-professional junior football had always been an essential part of the Scottish scene, with many clubs attracting high attendances and supplying talent to the very best teams north and south of the border.

SCOTLAND'S FIRST – AND ONLY – JUNIOR FOOTBALL MAGAZINE

the Game!

ISSUE 6
70 PENCE

Ian's dream!

NOAH ASH RECOVERY

SCOTTISH CUP 2ND ROUND SPECIAL

Right: The Football Association's own ideas for restructuring were articulated in its *Blueprint for the Future of Football*, which appeared in June 1991. Its suggestion of an FA-controlled Premier League led to the entire top division leaving the Football League within a couple of months.

Far right: The Football League's plan for the restructuring of football, *One Team, One Game, One Voice*, was launched in October 1990. It proposed a new system of power-sharing between the two.

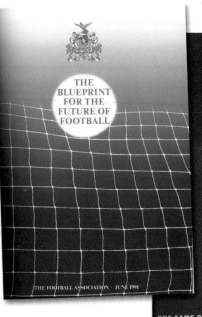

THE BLUEPRINT FOR THE FUTURE OF FOOTBALL

THE FOOTBALL ASSOCIATION · JUNE 1991

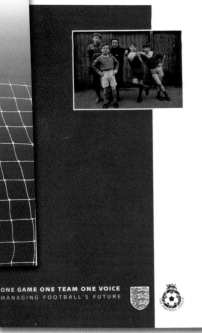

ONE GAME ONE TEAM ONE VOICE
MANAGING FOOTBALL'S FUTURE

Companies produced 'retro' football shirts and merchandise. Cups, pencil cases and other products featuring images from *Charles Buchan's Football Monthly* magazine and the table football game Subbuteo were sold in high street department stores. Successful museums were established by clubs such as Manchester United and Arsenal. The National Football Museum was opened in 2001, initially at Preston North End's Deepdale ground and then relocated to Manchester in 2011. Football had undergone a major transformation but much of its appeal to new and old fans alike lay in its history, heritage and traditions.